THE PINK PANTHER™

Story by
Len Blum and Michael Saltzman

Based on the screenplay by
Len Blum and Steve Martin

LEVEL 2

■SCHOLASTIC

Adapted by: Helen Parker

Commissioning Editor: Helen Parker

Editor: Diane Winkleby

Cover layout: Emily Spencer

Designer: Victoria Wren

Picture research: Emma Bree

Photo credits: Cover image and inside photos provided courtesy of Metro-Goldwyn-Mayer. **Page 50**: J. Eisele/AFP, S. Shugerman/Getty Images. **Page 51**: V. Roche/AFP, K. Winter/ Getty Images; Hemera. **Page 52**: S. Peterson/Getty Images; P. Behnke/Alamy; Hemera; Crown © / The Royal Collection © Her Majesty Queen Elizabeth II; Brand X.

CONTENTS

PAGE

THE PINK PANTHER™

The Police

< Inspector Jacques Clouseau is a very famous detective.

Inspector Dreyfus > is the Head of the French Police.

< Gilbert Ponton is Clouseau's deputy.

Agent Renard is Dreyfus's deputy.

The Dead Man

Yves Gluant is the French football team coach. He owns the Pink Panther diamond.

Nicole > works for Dreyfus and Clouseau.

The Suspects

Vainqueur is the deputy team coach of the French football team.

Yuri is the team trainer.

Raymond Larocque owns many restaurants and Larocque's Casino in Rome.

Doctor Li How Pang is the Head of Sports in China.

^ **Xania** is a very beautiful and famous singer.

Bizu is the star player of the French football team. >

Places

Paris is the biggest city in France. It is famous for the Eiffel Tower and the river Seine. The Palais de la Justice is the most important building of the French police. The Elysée Palace (or President's Palace) is the home of the President of France.

Rome is the most important city in Italy. Larocque's Casino is in Rome.

New York is the biggest city in the United States of America. The Waldorf Astoria is a famous hotel in New York.

Chapter 1
The football match

It was a big day – France was playing an important World Cup match against China. There was a large crowd watching the game. The crowd shouted and cheered very loudly.

The President of France and Inspector Dreyfus waited for the game to start. Inspector Dreyfus didn't care about football, but it was a great honour to watch the match with the President. And Dreyfus liked honours. Most of all he wanted the Medal of Honour*. For seven years he believed it was his. But they never gave it to him. 'This year is going to be different,' he thought.

Suddenly they heard, 'And now the coach of France – Yves Gluant!'

The crowd cheered loudly as the good-looking coach waved his hand. On his hand was a big pink diamond. The diamond was the Pink Panther, the most famous diamond in Europe.

Bizu, the star player, gave Gluant a look of hate. Gluant went to sit down next to his girlfriend, Xania. He took her in his arms and kissed her in front of everyone. Xania was a very famous and beautiful singer. Bizu hated Gluant because he wanted Xania to be his girlfriend.

At last the game started. First China scored a goal, and then France scored a goal. Then France scored, and then China scored. At the end of ninety minutes, they had to

* Medal of Honour: the highest honour in France.

continue playing. A minute before the end, Gluant told Jacquard, a young player, to go on. Then he took Bizu out of the game! Bizu was very angry. He ran to Gluant and shouted at him. Then he started to hit Gluant! The deputy coach had to stop him.

The game started again. At first the Chinese had the ball. Then Jacquard jumped, turned and scored with his head. It was fantastic! The crowd cheered and shouted. It was the end of the game, and the French were so happy. Many people ran to the French coach. Then suddenly, Gluant fell to the floor … He was dead.

The next day the story was in every newspaper:

FRENCH FOOTBALL COACH DEAD!

KILLER TAKES PINK PANTHER!

It was a very important time in Inspector Dreyfus's life. 'In three weeks they are going to decide about the Medal of Honour,' he thought. All around him there were large photos of Gluant's body and the Pink Panther diamond.

Agent Renard said, 'You'll get the Medal of Honour this time.'

But Dreyfus said, 'This is terrible. I can't take the Gluant case. They'll give the Medal of Honour to the Pink Panther detective. And what if I can't find the Pink Panther or the killer?

Then suddenly, he had a very good idea. 'I know what we need,' he said.

'What?' asked Agent Renard.

'We need someone very stupid … Yes, a very stupid detective! This detective will try very hard, but he will never find the killer. And the people from the TV and the newspapers will watch everything he does! Then I can take the best detectives in France and catch the killer myself.'

He looked at the big photo of the Pink Panther diamond and then he remembered. He turned to Agent Renard and said, 'I know the right man for the job. Find him and bring him to Paris. His name is … Jacques Clouseau.'

Chapter 2
Clouseau goes to Paris

A few days later, Clouseau left his small town to go to Paris. He looked at his map of France for a long time. He was very happy when he found Paris – and it wasn't far away. A few hours later, he drove past the famous river Seine. He drove past the Eiffel Tower … and out of Paris. A few miles later, he stopped the car. 'I've driven for hours,'

he thought. 'And I haven't seen one sign for Paris!'

Many hours later, Clouseau finally arrived at the Palais de la Justice. 'Lucky me!' he thought when he saw a parking place just outside the main entrance. First he crashed into the car in front. Then he crashed into the car behind. Happy with his parking, he went inside the building.

While Clouseau was parking, Inspector Dreyfus was in his office. He was telling his secret team of detectives about the Gluant case.

'The killer used a poison dart from China,' he said. 'Anyone in the area close to Gluant could be the killer – perhaps one of the players or someone from the newspapers. Maybe Bizu or Xania. Or, perhaps somebody shot the dart from the crowd.'

He turned to his deputy and said, 'Renard, you and your men will look carefully at the video of the match. Find all the possible suspects and question them. Then find every business in China making poison darts. Look carefully at their order books.'

Then he told another detective to find more information about Gluant. 'Find out where Gluant went every day and what he did,' he said. 'Find everyone he met and find out if anyone hated him.'

Clouseau arrived outside Dreyfus's office just as the detectives were leaving.

'One moment, please,' said a pretty woman called Nicole. She was standing on a desk. She was trying to hang a very large picture of her boss, Inspector Dreyfus.

She smiled at Clouseau and offered her hand. He took her hand and helped her to get off the desk. A moment later, one of Dreyfus's detectives arrived. He was a little surprised to see Clouseau holding Nicole's hand.

'Erm… Inspector Dreyfus will see you now,' he said.

'Jacques Clouseau, police officer third class!' Clouseau said as he went into Dreyfus's office.

Dreyfus started to speak, but Clouseau started to walk around the room.

'YES, WE ARE HAVING WONDERFUL WEATHER … I HOPE THE WEATHER CONTINUES!' he said very loudly.

Clouseau then started to search the room. He looked everywhere. Finally, he looked behind the curtains and said, 'No one is listening. The area is safe.'

'Clouseau, I have heard many stories about you and your work,' Dreyfus said. 'You are a brilliant police officer, and you are ready for a much higher job. I have decided to make you an Inspector – the highest job in the French police.'

'Inspector!' said Clouseau. He was very happy, but also a little surprised.

'Yes,' said Dreyfus as he tried to hide a smile. 'Your first job will be the Gluant case. You will catch the killer and find the Pink Panther diamond.'

Then Dreyfus took a piece of paper and a pen. He signed the paper and said, 'You are now a full Inspector of the French police.'

'It is a great honour,' said Clouseau.

'Now you are going to meet the people from the TV and newspapers. They are waiting for you downstairs. Good luck!' Dreyfus said.

As he went to the door, Clouseau looked behind the curtains again. The curtains crashed to the floor. 'The area is safe,' said Clouseau.

'Yes,' Dreyfus said to himself. 'I think we've found the right man!'

Chapter 3
Is the killer Chinese?

An excited crowd of people from the TV and newspapers was waiting for Clouseau. Everyone wanted to ask him questions about the Gluant case.

A good-looking woman asked, 'How will you catch the killer, Inspector?'

'First I will have an idea. Then I will have some more ideas … ,' he answered.

Many other people put up their hands to ask a question. But Clouseau only wanted to answer the good-looking woman's questions.

Finally, a man was able to ask, 'Do you think the killer is watching you now?'

'Yes, I'm sure the killer is watching,' Clouseau said. 'And I have a message for the killer …'

Clouseau turned suddenly and looked at the TV cameras.

'There is nowhere you can hide. Killer, I will find you! Because I am Inspector Clouseau … Because detectives are detectives … And France is France!'

Many people cheered. The room was full of lights as the photographers took pictures. But one person wasn't happy. Inspector Dreyfus didn't like all the interest in Clouseau. No, he didn't like it one little bit.

Later that day, Nicole showed Clouseau his new office. He sat down at his desk and took a hair from his head. He put the hair very carefully in the desk.

'Now you are Inspector Clouseau, so you'll need some new clothes,' Nicole said. 'I'll get some for you.'

Just then a man arrived at the door. He was quite a big man with a friendly smile.

'Gilbert Ponton,' he said. 'Detective, second class. I'm your new deputy.'

Dreyfus and his secret team of detectives were watching the video of the match. Just after Gluant fell to the floor, the camera moved back to show the crowd.

'Stop the video there!' Dreyfus ordered. He said, 'Look at these angry Chinese people. One of them could be the killer. Perhaps one of them shot the poison dart. And the poison dart was, of course, Chinese. Did Gluant ever go to China?'

'Three years ago he took some French players to Beijing for a match,' one of the detectives answered.

'I'm not sure, but I think the killer is Chinese,' Dreyfus said.

He ordered one of the detectives to go to Beijing. Then he turned to another and said, 'Find out about those Chinese people in the crowd.'

As the team of detectives left the room, Renard came to Dreyfus. He said 'Ponton just called. Clouseau is getting nowhere.'

Dreyfus looked a little happier. 'That's good news,' he said.

Chapter 4
Clouseau meets Xania

Clouseau and Ponton went to meet their first suspect. Soon they arrived at the place where Xania was making her new CD. Clouseau pushed his way into the room. Inside, a large group of people was playing music. Clouseau pushed through them. Then he walked up to a small room at the back where Xania was singing. Clouseau started to question her. But Xania had her eyes closed. She couldn't hear a thing!

Suddenly, a man came out of another small room. He was very angry and shouted, 'Stop! Stop!' The music stopped and the man asked Clouseau, 'Who are you? What are you doing?'

Clouseau was a little upset. He answered, 'I am Inspector Clouseau. I am working on an important case.'

A moment later, Xania came out and said to the man, 'It's OK.' Then she turned to Clouseau and gave him a lovely smile. Clouseau's mouth fell open. 'She's the most

beautiful woman I've ever seen,' he thought. He looked deep into her eyes …

Ponton decided to continue with the questions.

'You were near Gluant when he died,' he said to Xania.

'Yes,' she answered. 'I ran to him when the team won.'

Clouseau gave her a loving look. Then he said, 'A few hours before the match, six people saw you … You were hitting Gluant and you were shouting … What was it, Ponton?'

'"I'm going to kill you! I'm going to kill you!"' Ponton said.

'I was very angry,' Xania explained. 'I found him with another woman.'

'You poor little thing,' answered Clouseau softly.

'Yes, I hated him for that, but I didn't kill him,' she continued.

'I know you didn't,' Clouseau said, looking into her beautiful face.

'Have you ever sung in China?' Ponton asked.

'Yes, three months ago in Shanghai,' she answered.

'Did anyone else hate Gluant?' Clouseau asked.

'Bizu,' Xania said. 'I was going out with Bizu when I met Gluant. He hated Gluant for going out with me.'

Finally, Clouseau said to Xania, 'Don't leave Paris!'

She looked away for a moment. Then she answered, 'Next week I have … erm … something to do in New York.'

Clouseau smiled and said, 'Well … erm … That's OK. You can go where you want!'

Clouseau looked at Xania once more. Then he turned and left the room.

Chapter 5
Did Bizu kill Gluant?

Clouseau and Ponton went to see their next suspect – Bizu. They arrived at the French football team building. Inside, a young woman, Cherie, was there to meet them.

'I'm sorry, but Bizu isn't able to see you,' she said. 'You can speak to Vainqueur, the deputy coach … Well, he's the main coach now.'

She took Clouseau and Ponton to meet Vainqueur in the training room.

'I'm Inspector Clouseau. Perhaps you have heard of me?'

'No,' said Vainqueur. 'What do you want?'

'I believe Bizu hated Gluant,' Clouseau said.

'A lot of people hated Gluant,' Vainqueur answered.

'Did you?' Clouseau asked.

'I worked for him for six years. Every day for six years he was horrible to me,' said Vainqueur. 'I didn't like Yves Gluant one little bit.'

'Now he's dead, and you have his job – a bit strange, don't you think?'

'It's not always sad when some people die,' he answered.

At that moment a short, strong-looking man came into the room.

'Who are you?' Clouseau asked.

'I'm Yuri, the trainer,' he answered.

'And what do you do here?'

'I'm the trainer,' Yuri said again.

Clouseau didn't believe him. 'Yuri, the trainer and you train!' he said with a laugh.

Yuri left the room, and Clouseau turned again to Vainqueur.

'And what about Bizu?' Clouseau asked. 'Did he hate Gluant?'

'Yes, he did,' answered Vainqueur.

'Where is Bizu now?'

'He's practising outside,' Vainqueur said.

'Well,' said Clouseau. 'Let's ask Bizu some questions …'

In a small room in the Palais de la Justice, Bizu was sitting in a hard chair. Under the strong lights, Clouseau was questioning him. He was playing at 'good cop*, bad cop'.

'Did you know Yves Gluant?' Clouseau shouted.

'Yes,' Bizu answered angrily.

'Did you hate him?'

'Yes!'

'Did you kill him?' he asked.

'I wanted to kill him, but another lucky person did it first!'

'You make me ill!' said Clouseau. And suddenly he left the room.

* *cop = police officer*

Moments later Clouseau came back. This time he was nice and friendly.

'Bizu, I know you didn't do it,' he said with a smile.

'Good!' Bizu said. He was a little surprised.

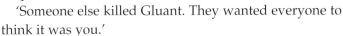

'Someone else killed Gluant. They wanted everyone to think it was you.'

'Will you help me?' Bizu asked.

'Yes, I'll help you. But, who do you think killed Gluant?'

'His business partner in those stupid restaurants – Larocque,' said Bizu.

'Raymond Larocque, the owner of Larocque's Casino?' Clouseau asked.

'Yes! Gluant took money from the restaurants and spent it all in the casino,' said Bizu. 'Larocque was so angry with him … I think he wanted to kill Gluant!'

While Clouseau was questioning Bizu, Dreyfus was watching the news with Renard. Clouseau's face suddenly appeared on the TV.

'They are already calling him the Pink Panther detective,' the newsreader said. 'And he has brought new hope to the people of France ...'

Dreyfus turned off the TV. He was very worried.

'Perhaps Clouseau isn't the most stupid detective after all,' he said to Renard.

Chapter 6
'Oh, it's you!'

When Clouseau arrived at his flat, he saw something strange. The front door was open a little bit. He took out his gun and started looking closely at the door. Suddenly it closed – on Clouseau's fingers. He fell to the floor. Then he shot his gun at the door, but the gun was empty. A moment later the door opened and Nicole was standing there.

'I'm very sorry,' she said. 'I just came to give you your new clothes.'

Clouseau's hand hurt. Nicole asked, 'Would you like some cold water?'

'Yes, please,' said Clouseau.

They both went inside the flat and Nicole went to get the water from the fridge.

Just then Ponton arrived. He was a bit surprised to see Nicole in Clouseau's flat.

'What is it, Ponton?' asked Clouseau.

'Bizu is dead! He was in the changing room. The killer

shot him in the head,' Ponton answered.

Clouseau started walking around the room. 'I want to talk to Bizu now,' he said.

'But he's dead,' said Ponton.

'Ah! Good point,' said Clouseau. 'Was anyone there when he died?'

'Yes – just one person.'

It was dark when they arrived at the French football team building. They found Cherie in the changing room.

'Please tell me what you saw,' Clouseau said.

'Well, I didn't see anything,' Cherie said, 'I was going past the changing room when I heard sounds inside. I heard Bizu say, "Oh, it's you!" And then the sound of a gun.'

Clouseau pulled Ponton to one side. He told him, 'Find everyone in Paris with the name "You". I want to question them.'

He looked at the floor of the changing room. There was a white line around Bizu's body.

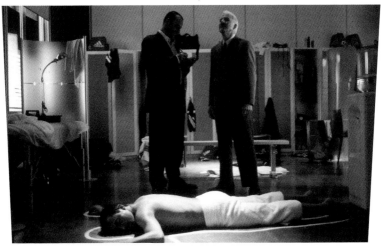

'Ponton,' said Clouseau, 'Isn't that clever? The body fell exactly inside that white line.'

'I think they drew the line later,' Ponton said, but Clouseau wasn't listening.

'Yes, we are looking for a highly intelligent killer,' said Clouseau. 'Ponton, we are going to talk to this man, Raymond Larocque. Where is his casino?'

'It's in the beautiful city of Rome,' Ponton answered.

Chapter 7
When in Rome ...

Late that night, Clouseau and Ponton arrived outside Larocque's Casino. They got out of Clouseau's little car and went into the building.

Inside the casino, people in expensive clothes were playing games around large tables. Beautiful waitresses with drinks moved through the crowd.

'Ponton, go and find Larocque's office,' said Clouseau, 'I'll wait here.'

Clouseau looked at the people in the room. Just then Clouseau heard a good-looking man say very loudly, 'IT'S NICE WEATHER WE'RE HAVING. I HOPE THE WEATHER CONTINUES.'

Clouseau moved close to the good-looking man. 'I'm in police work, too,' he said very quietly.

The man looked a little uncomfortable. 'Is it so easy to tell?' he asked.

'No,' Clouseau answered, 'I'm just good at these things.'

Just then a waitress brought the man a drink. The man said, 'Light it.'

For a few moments, the drink was on fire.

'That's brilliant,' said Clouseau. 'I will remember that.'

Then he said very quietly, 'I am Inspector Clouseau. I'm here on a very important case.'

'I am Nigel Boswell,' the man answered. 'I'm Agent 006. I'm on an important case, too. But I'm not here – I'm in Switzerland.'

'You're not here – you're in Switzerland,' Clouseau said.

'No one must know I'm here,' Boswell explained.

'I've put my mobile phone number in your pocket,' Clouseau said. 'Call me if you need anything …'

Clouseau met Ponton in Larocque's office. Moments later, they were inside Larocque's very large and comfortable flat. A thin man nearly sixty years old was watching Clouseau. But Clouseau didn't see him. He was too interested in the pictures on the walls. There were works by Monet, Renoir, Gauguin …

The man moved towards Clouseau and said, 'I'm Raymond Larocque. How can I help you?'

'I'm trying to find the

killer of Yves Gluant,' Clouseau said.

'Ah, yes, Yves … a very interesting man,' said Larocque.

'You were his business partner in the restaurants,' said Clouseau. 'Gluant is dead so you must be much richer now.'

'Richer! How am I much richer?'

'Now you own all the restaurants,' Clouseau said.

'The restaurants were a terrible mistake!' Larocque shouted. 'Gluant spent all the money we made. There was only one good thing – he spent all the money in my casino. But in the end he lost so badly, he had to offer me the Pink Panther …'

Just then, there was a call on Clouseau's mobile phone. He looked for a long time in his coat pockets for the phone. When he finally answered, he said, 'Well, yes … I can meet you. In the restaurant? Yes, right away!'

Without another word, Clouseau turned and left the flat.

Boswell was waiting for Clouseau in the dark, empty restaurant.

'Clouseau!' Boswell said. 'I need your help. Look behind you.'

Clouseau looked through the window. Down on the floor below, some men in masks were taking all the money from the tables in the Casino.

'They are the Masked Bandits,' Boswell explained. 'Everyone in Europe is looking for them.'

'I am ready,' Clouseau said. 'How can I help?'

'I need your coat,' answered Boswell.

'Why?' asked Clouseau.

'No one must know I am here – remember!' Boswell said, 'But I can't let the Masked Bandits escape!'

Boswell put on Clouseau's coat and a mask. Then he

took out a special cutter. He cut a hole in the glass and went through the window. He went down to the casino floor and took out his gun. He arrested the Masked Bandits and was back in the restaurant in a minute.

Quickly he gave Clouseau his coat, the mask and the glass cutter. And a second later, he disappeared.

Suddenly, a crowd of people ran into the restaurant.

'That was fantastic!' said an inspector from the Italian police.

Clouseau smiled a big smile as the photographers took his picture for the newspapers.

Chapter 8
How much does Clouseau know?

The next morning, there were photos of Clouseau on the front page of every newspaper. But he didn't have time to stop and enjoy the moment.

When he arrived at work, Ponton was waiting for him.

'We have found all the people in Paris with the name

"You",' he told Clouseau.

'Now we're getting somewhere,' said Clouseau.

Ponton took Clouseau to the small room where a Mrs Yu was waiting.

Under the strong lights Clouseau asked, 'Where were you when Gluant died?'

Mrs Yu gave a very long answer in Chinese.

Clouseau closed his eyes for a second. Then he said, 'You can go.'

'Do you speak Chinese?' asked Ponton.

'Of course I speak Chinese!' Clouseau said angrily. 'Do you really think I don't speak Chinese? Inspector Clouseau does not speak Chinese?! How could I not speak Chinese?!'

While Clouseau and Ponton were busy with Mrs Yu, Dreyfus decided to search Clouseau's office. All morning, people from the newspapers were asking, 'Are the Masked Bandits suspects in the Gluant case?' Dreyfus was upset about all the interest in Clouseau. 'How much does Clouseau really know?' he thought to himself.

Dreyfus sat down at Clouseau's desk. He started to look through Clouseau's things. He opened an address book. It was full of the names of famous girl singers. Just then he heard Clouseau – he was coming back to his office.

Dreyfus looked around for a place to hide and then went behind the curtains.

A moment later, Clouseau came into the room. He felt that something was wrong. He looked for the hair in his desk. It wasn't there! 'Now I know someone has searched my things!' he said to himself.

Clouseau looked around the room. He stopped at the

curtains and looked down. He could see a pair of men's shoes under the curtains.

'Nicole,' Clouseau called, 'can I see you now?'

When Nicole came into the room, Clouseau was holding a chair.

'Ah, Nicole. THE WEATHER IS SO NICE. DO YOU THINK IT IS GOING TO STAY THIS WARM … ?'

WHAM! Clouseau hit the curtains with the chair. The man fell to the floor and the curtains fell on top of him. Then, Nicole gave lots of heavy things to Clouseau. Clouseau used them to hit the man.

After that, they went behind Clouseau's desk and together they pushed it into him. WHAM!

'Right,' said Clouseau. 'Let's see who you are!'

Clouseau lifted the curtains. The man looked just like Inspector Dreyfus!

'That's terrible!' shouted Clouseau. 'Did you think you could trick me with that Dreyfus mask?'

Clouseau tried and tried to pull off the mask. He pulled Dreyfus around his office by his face, but the mask didn't move.

A little later, Clouseau went to see Dreyfus. He was sitting on his desk. He was holding something cold against his face.

'I am so sorry, Inspector,' Clouseau said.

'Let's forget about it,' said Dreyfus. He quickly moved his desk between him and the dangerous Clouseau.

'Would you like to know how I'm doing with the Gluant case?'

'Yes,' said Dreyfus, 'How many suspects are there now?'

'27,683,' said Clouseau.

'27,683!' said Dreyfus.

Dreyfus was so happy. 'Clouseau is as stupid as I thought,' he said to himself. 'In just a few more days the Medal of Honour will be mine.'

Chapter 9
New York, New York!

Later that afternoon, Ponton found Clouseau. He was walking home to his flat along the Seine.

'Can we discuss the case?' said Ponton.

'Good idea, Ponton. Now then, what are the facts?'

'Someone killed Yves Gluant with a poison dart at the France-China game. Bizu wanted to kill him, but is now dead. Gluant was taking money from Larocque. And Xania was next to Gluant when he died,' said Ponton.

'I want her!' Clouseau cried.

'What?' said Ponton.

'Nothing,' said Clouseau quickly. 'So who do you think killed Yves Gluant?'

'I think Xania is the killer,' Ponton answered.

'Oh no, my poor little deputy – Xania isn't the killer,' said Clouseau.

'Xania is the killer!' Ponton cried. He was no longer able to hide his real thoughts. 'I like you and I'm trying to help you. You only think like this because you're in love with her!'

'Xania isn't the killer,' said Clouseau, 'but she knows more than she is saying. Where is she now?'

'She left suddenly for New York,' Ponton told him.

'And where is this New York?' asked Clouseau.

'In the United States of America,' Ponton explained.

'Well, Ponton, we are going to follow her to New York,' said Clouseau, 'and find out what she is doing there.'

When Clouseau and Ponton arrived in New York, the first thing they did was buy some hamburgers.

'Hello,' Clouseau said to the hamburger seller. 'I would like to buy a *damburger*.' He tried to sound like a New Yorker and gave a big American smile.

The seller just looked at Clouseau and smiled back. Clouseau's English sounded so terrible, he couldn't understand a word.

Early the next morning Clouseau and Ponton waited outside the Waldorf Astoria, the hotel where Xania was staying.

Suddenly, Xania walked out of the hotel.

'There she is!' said Clouseau. 'Let's follow her.'

Clouseau and Ponton followed Xania down the street. When she looked back, they held newspapers in front of their faces.

They followed Xania to an old building. She looked both ways, then went into the building.

'Newspapers!' cried Clouseau. He didn't see the stairs down to a train station.

'Ahhhhggghhh!' he shouted as he fell down the stairs.

When Clouseau and Ponton finally went into the building, Xania disappeared into a lift.

At last, they found Xania in a large room at the top of the building. At the back of the room there was a man. He was sitting at a desk and was cutting something. Xania was standing near him.

'Stop!' cried Clouseau and walked towards them. 'I am Inspector Clouseau of the French police. What are you cutting?'

'A diamond,' said the man.

Ponton looked very closely at the diamond. 'It isn't the Pink Panther,' he said.

'You're right, it isn't the Pink Panther,' the man said.

'And what are you doing here?' Clouseau said as he turned to Xania.

She showed him a small bag. The outside of the bag was covered in diamonds.

'I'm singing at the party at the President's Palace tomorrow night. I wanted my bag to look really special with lots of diamonds,' Xania explained.

'Why didn't you tell me about this?' Clouseau asked.

'I couldn't tell anyone after what happened to the Pink Panther … ,' Xania explained.

Just then, there was a phone call. The diamond cutter tried to reach the phone, but Clouseau stopped him. The caller left a message.

'The "cat" is out of the bag,' said a strange man's voice. 'You are the world's greatest "trainer" and in time it will come to you. Call me.'

'Who was that?' asked Ponton.

'I don't know,' said the diamond cutter. 'Many people call here.'

'I think the caller has the Pink Panther,' said Ponton.

'Ponton!' Clouseau said, 'My funny, sweet Ponton. He was just talking about a cat.'

When they finished, Clouseau and Ponton went with Xania to the Waldorf hotel.

As they walked along, Clouseau asked, 'When are you leaving New York?'

'Tomorrow,' Xania answered. Then she turned to

Clouseau and asked, 'Would you like to have dinner with me tonight, Inspector?'

'Of course!' Clouseau answered. 'At what time?'

'Eight o'clock in my room on the second floor,' she said. Then she turned and walked away.

'Perhaps it's a trick,' Ponton said.

Clouseau smiled and said, 'Perhaps … but a nice trick.'

Chapter 10

Dinner with Xania

That evening, Clouseau met Xania in her comfortable hotel room. They ordered some drinks. Clouseau remembered Boswell. He told the waiter to light his drink.

The Inspector couldn't take his eyes off the beautiful singer.

'Why?' Clouseau asked as he looked at Xania over the fire on his drink.

'Why what?' said Xania.

'Why did you keep your visit today so secret?'

'I was frightened of Larocque. I thought, "Perhaps

he will follow me to New York",' Xania explained.

'Larocque?' Clouseau asked, surprised.

'He wants to kill the person with the Pink Panther. He believes the Pink Panther is his,' said Xania. 'My visit today could give the wrong idea.'

'You know,' said Clouseau, 'a man sitting

here in your hotel room could get the wrong idea, too.'

'Or the right one,' said Xania. She looked into Clouseau's eyes. 'I have heard things about you.'

'Really?' said Clouseau. He tried to look cool as he drank some of his drink. Suddenly, his hair caught fire. But Clouseau didn't see or feel anything.

'Excuse me one moment. I just need to go to the bathroom,' he said.

Clouseau got up from the sofa with his drink in his hand. He walked very slowly to the bathroom – he still couldn't take his eyes off Xania.

Inside the bathroom, he looked at himself in the mirror. And suddenly he saw that his hair was on fire. Quickly he threw the drink on the floor. Then he hit his hair with his hands to stop the fire.

When he returned to Xania, she smiled and said, 'You like to make a girl wait.'

'It's all part of the plan,' said Clouseau.

He sat down next to Xania, then moved closer to her … He was going to kiss her.

Suddenly they heard, 'THERE'S A FIRE IN THE BUILDING! LEAVE THE BUILDING NOW!'

Clouseau and Xania jumped up from the sofa. Then Clouseau took Xania's hand, and they ran out of the hotel together.

Outside the hotel they waited for the fire fighters to put out the fire.

'I forgot to ask,' said Clouseau to Xania. 'What time does your plane leave tomorrow?'

'Ten o'clock in the morning,' she answered.

'See you at the airport!' said Clouseau.

Very late that night in Paris, Dreyfus was at his desk. He was finishing a very secret phone call …

'Yes, I know what time he's leaving New York tomorrow. He'll be there before 10 o'clock in the morning. Just look for the most stupid man at the airport …'

The next morning, a man moved very quietly through the crowd at the airport. He had a bag exactly the same as Clouseau's. As Clouseau waited in line to go through the x-ray machine, the man changed his bag with Clouseau's. Then the man disappeared into the crowd.

Ponton joined Clouseau in the line. Clouseau looked around, then said very quietly, 'Did you get them?'

'Yes,' Ponton answered.

Ponton opened his bag and took out two hamburgers. Very slowly and carefully, Clouseau took the hamburgers and put them into his coat pocket.

'The food on the plane is terrible. No one will see,' said Clouseau.

Just then, there were lots of lights from cameras and cries of 'Xania! Xania! Over here!' Clouseau and Ponton turned and saw Xania. There were photographers all around her.

'OK. Let's go. Next!' said the man at the x-ray machine.

Clouseau moved forward and put his bag on the machine. A few moments later, two men stopped Clouseau and took his bag from the x-ray machine. One of the men started to open the bag. Suddenly, the photographers lost interest in Xania and ran over to Clouseau.

The man took out … a small pink pocket knife!

'Oh, please!' said Clouseau, almost laughing, 'It's just a pocket knife!'

The man put the knife on the table. Then he put his hand in the bag and pulled out … a gun!

Clouseau looked very surprised. 'That's strange,' he said.

Then, the man pulled out … a great big gun!

Clouseau couldn't believe it. A crowd of people stopped to watch.

Then the man pulled out … an even bigger gun!

'Ooooh!' said the crowd. There were lots of lights as the photographers took pictures.

Moments later some police officers with dogs came over. One of the dogs smelled the hamburgers. Clouseau tried to push the dog away, but it started to jump up at his pocket. Clouseau shouted at the dog and put his hand in his pocket to save the hamburgers. But it looked like he had a gun.

'What's in your pocket?' asked one of the police officers.

'Nothing!' Clouseau answered.

'I'll ask you again,' said the officer. 'What's in your pocket?'

'OK. Fine. It's a *damburger*.'

'What?!' cried the man angrily.

'A *damburger*. You know? A *damburger*?'

One of the police officers quickly picked up a radio and started to shout, 'We've got a *damburger* on six! *Damburger* on six!'

Suddenly a group of men with big guns ran up to Clouseau. They pointed their guns in his face. Then, the police officer let his dog go, and it jumped on Clouseau. WHAM! Clouseau hit the floor.

CLICK! CLICK! FLASH! The world's photographers were there to take the picture.

Chapter 11
Doctor Li How Pang

Back in Paris, Dreyfus was only hours away from arresting the killer. He now had all the facts. And the facts pointed to one man …

'Meet Doctor Li How Pang,' Dreyfus said to his team. He pointed to a large photo of Doctor Pang on the wall of his office. 'He is the Head of Sports in China. He was at the match when Gluant died. Gluant had some meetings with Pang when he was in Beijing.' Dreyfus pointed to some large photos of Gluant in China.

He continued, 'Pang was taking money from Chinese sports and sending it to Gluant. Pang wanted Gluant to put the money into a European bank. But Gluant spent the money in Larocque's Casino. Pang was really angry, but he couldn't say anything – in China they often kill people who take the country's money. Instead, Doctor Li How Pang killed Yves Gluant.'

Dreyfus turned to his detectives and said, 'Doctor Pang is in Paris for the President's party. We will arrest him there tonight!'

The detectives cheered very loudly. Just then, Renard ran into the office. He was holding a newspaper.

'Have you seen this?' he asked and he showed Dreyfus the front page:

CLOUSEAU ARRESTED AT AIRPORT

Dreyfus tried to hide a great big smile. 'This is terribly sad,' he said. But really he was thinking, 'At last Clouseau has made a big mistake! And now I have found the killer – the Medal of Honour will be mine!'

Moments later a police car arrived outside the Palais de la Justice. The police took Clouseau to a small room in the Palais.

In the small room Inspector Dreyfus, Renard, Ponton and some other detectives stood around Clouseau. Under the strong lights, Dreyfus questioned him about his arrest at the airport. When he finished, he looked at Clouseau and said,

'Well, Clouseau, today is a great day for France. A stupid man with the name Clouseau is going to become an ordinary policeman.'

'You have another Clouseau?'

'I'm talking about you, you stupid man,' Dreyfus cried. 'Understand this, Clouseau. I didn't make you an Inspector because you were a good detective. It was because you were the most stupid police officer in all of France!'

Clouseau couldn't believe it. 'But what about all my good points?'

'What good points?' Dreyfus said. 'I gave you the job so you could make a big mistake. Then I could take over the Gluant case.'

'I was only trying to catch a killer,' Clouseau told him sadly.

'You were trying to become famous,' Dreyfus answered. 'Now you can go and read all the bad stories about you in the newspapers. Goodbye, Clouseau!'

Dreyfus turned to leave. Renard asked, 'Do you want me to lock him away?'

'No,' said Dreyfus. 'Let him go back home to his small town and his ordinary life.'

Later that afternoon, Ponton drove Clouseau to his flat.

'I'm sorry, Inspector,' Ponton said. 'I didn't know Dreyfus was using you like that.'

'I was stupid, Ponton,' Clouseau answered. 'Sorry if I made you look stupid.'

'It was an honour working with you,' Ponton said.

Clouseau smiled at Ponton sadly; then he turned and went into his flat.

Inside the flat, Clouseau started to think, 'Something isn't quite right …' He sat down at his computer. 'Ah, the Internet! Hello, old friend!' he said.

He opened the news page. At the top of the page he read:

INSPECTOR CLOUSEAU LOSES JOB

Under this was a photo of his arrest at the airport. He looked away for a moment – it hurt to remember! Then he looked again at the photo.

Just then, he saw something. He made that part of the picture bigger. He couldn't believe his eyes! He ran to the phone and called Ponton.

'Ponton!' he cried. 'Come to my flat right now!'

Then he called Nicole.

'Nicole,' he said. 'When you go to the party tonight, bring me my bag with "President's Palace" on it. I'll meet you there. Hurry!'

Moments later, Ponton arrived outside the flat. Clouseau jumped into the car. 'Ponton, we must go to the President's Palace right now,' he cried.

Ponton shouted to Clouseau, 'What is this all about?'

'The same person killed Gluant and Bizu. And that person is going to kill again tonight!' Clouseau shouted back.

'But Bizu's killer used a gun,' Ponton shouted. 'And Gluant's killer used a Chinese poison dart.'

'Sometimes I like meat, and sometimes I like fish,' Clouseau answered. 'The killer wants us to think there are two different killers. Now we have to ask, "Who joins the two cases together?"'

'Xania?' Ponton guessed.

'Exactly.'

'She killed them?'

'No, Ponton!' cried Clouseau. 'Xania is the next to die!'

Chapter 12
Xania sings

That evening the President's Palace was full of activity. People were hurrying to get everything ready for the party. Dreyfus stood at the main entrance with one of his men.

'Don't let Clouseau in,' he said. 'He has lost his job and he is not welcome at the party.'

'And what about all the people from the TV and newspapers?' the man asked.

'When the time is right, let them all in,' Dreyfus said. He wanted them to see the special moment – the arrest of Gluant's killer.

It was dark when Clouseau and Ponton arrived at the President's Palace. They parked the car and hurried to the main entrance. A woman at the door said, 'I'm sorry but you can't come in.'

Clouseau and Ponton walked back down the stairs and looked for another entrance.

Just then they heard a sound like a bird's call. Clouseau looked around and saw Nicole. She was waving at them from behind the building. They ran to meet her.

'Inspector, here is your bag,' she said. 'And I brought these – the plans of the President's Palace.'

'Good work,' said Clouseau.

'What's in the bag?' asked Ponton.

'Special clothes – no one will see us in these,' Clouseau answered.

'Go!' said Nicole.

Inside the President's Palace, everyone was enjoying

the party. Men and women in beautiful clothes talked
and drank. Doctor Pang moved through the crowd with
his men around him. Dreyfus watched Pang very closely.
Then he turned to Renard and said, 'Pang's in the room.
We'll arrest him in ten minutes.'

In a dressing room, Xania was nearly ready to sing.
She was sitting in front of a large mirror. She was putting
make-up on her face. She looked into the mirror and saw
the door open behind her. Larocque came into the room.
Xania put down her make-up.

'I know you killed Gluant,' Larocque said. His voice
was cold and hard.

'Don't be stupid,' Xania answered quickly.

'Believe me, I don't care,' he said. 'I hated him. But the
Pink Panther is mine.'

'But I don't have it,' Xania told him. 'And why is it
yours?'

'Because I want it. And I always get what I want,' he said.

He touched Xania's face and said, 'Remember – bad things can happen to beautiful people.'

He gave Xania a strange smile. Xania looked back at him. She was very frightened.

Just then the lights went down, and it was time for her to sing. She took her special bag and left the room.

The crowd cheered when Xania appeared. She was sitting behind a long white curtain. The curtain went up, and she started to sing.

Clouseau and Ponton were watching, but no one could see them. They were wearing the special clothes. The front of the clothes was the same colour as the curtains. The back of the clothes was the same as the walls.

Clouseau moved along the curtain until he reached the wall. Then he turned over and moved along the wall. When he reached the next curtain, he turned again.

Ponton was close behind Clouseau. He was moving

around the room in the same way.

Finally, they reached an open door and ran through it.

Just then they heard a sound, and they saw a man. He was dressed in black and was wearing a black mask. He ran out through a door.

'There's the killer. After him!' shouted Clouseau.

But suddenly they heard, 'STOP! PUT YOUR HANDS UP!'

It was one of Dreyfus's men, and he was pointing a gun at them!

A second later, a door opened and Nicole ran in. For a moment she looked very surprised, but then she said very quickly, 'You two! Where were you? The show starts in five minutes!'

'You know these two?' said the man.

'Of course! They're Xania's dancers. Why do you think they're dressed like that?'

The man thought for a moment. Then he said, 'OK. So you are dancers. Show me!'

Clouseau and Ponton started to dance. At first they were very slow and uncomfortable, but then they started to enjoy themselves. They ended their dance with big smiles and open arms.

The man looked at them for a moment, then started to cheer. 'Very good,' he said. 'Well done!'

'Can't you see these dancers are thirsty?' said Nicole quickly. 'Get them some water!'

The man hurried out of the room to get the water. Clouseau and Ponton put on black clothes and masks.

'Nicole, you were brilliant!' said Clouseau.

He moved closer to Nicole. They looked deep into each other's eyes. Nicole waited for her kiss, but …

'Ahem, Inspector, the killer,' said Ponton.

'Oh! Right! We must hurry, Ponton,' said Clouseau.

'You go downstairs and watch Xania. We've got a killer to catch.'

Clouseau and Ponton ran out of the door.

But a moment later, Clouseau was back. He took Nicole in his arms and gave her a great big kiss. It was true love!

Clouseau and Ponton ran up the stairs to the next floor.

'Inspector, look!' cried Ponton. He pointed up at a small window at the top of the building. Through the window they could see the man. He was looking down at Xania below. He was going to shoot her!

'This way!' cried Ponton. They climbed through the small window and onto the top of the building. The man turned around. He was completely surprised to see the two men in black. He ran away as fast as he could.

'You go that way, and I'll go this way,' said Clouseau.

Soon Ponton could see the killer. He was running towards a door. He tried to go through the door, but it was locked. Ponton took out his gun and pointed it at him.

'Turn around and put your hands behind your head!' Ponton shouted as he moved nearer to the killer.

Suddenly a door opened and hit Ponton in the face. He fell to the floor – he couldn't move.

'What are you doing on the floor, Ponton? This is no time for sleeping!' said Clouseau.

Then Clouseau saw the killer. He turned around to face him. It was one on one.

The killer took a sword from the wall and pointed it at Clouseau. Clouseau also took a sword and pointed it at the killer.

'Give up now and save yourself – I'm the greatest sword-fighter in all of France,' cried Clouseau.

TINK! With a simple move of his hand, the killer hit Clouseau's sword and it fell to the floor.

'Uh-oh,' said Clouseau. 'Good one!'

WHOOSH! The killer moved his sword very quickly past Clouseau's head. Clouseau jumped back just in time.

'You know, perhaps we could try something else? Sword-fighting isn't very popular these days.'

The killer moved his sword again. And again Clouseau jumped away just in time.

'How about a game of Snap* … ?'

The killer moved his sword once more. Clouseau jumped back. This time he fell over Ponton's body onto the floor.

Now, with no one in his way, the killer quickly dropped the sword and ran off.

Chapter 13
Chinese herbs

Back at the party, Xania was finishing her song. Dreyfus looked at his watch. It was time …

'Now we will make the arrest,' he said very quietly to his men.

When Xania finished the song, the crowd shouted and cheered. Dreyfus and his men moved across the room. Suddenly, all the doors were open and all the people from the TV and newspapers came into the room.

'Now!' shouted Dreyfus.

The men took out their guns and stood around Doctor Pang.

Dreyfus came forward. 'Well, Doctor Pang, you wanted the French police to look stupid. But in the name of

Snap – a children's game

France, I am arresting you. You are the killer of Yves Gluant!'

The crowd in the room cheered, and there were lots of lights as the photographers took pictures.

Just then, the masked man ran into the room with Clouseau and Ponton right behind him.

'Arrest Clouseau!' ordered Dreyfus.

'But which one is Clouseau?' he thought. The three masked men all looked the same.

The first man turned and ran down some stairs. The second man followed. The third man also went down the stairs but fell on the way down.

'That's him!' cried Dreyfus.

WHAM! Clouseau fell on top of the killer. The killer fell to the floor. Clouseau jumped up and pulled off his own mask. 'In the name of France, I am arresting you. You are the killer of Yves Gluant, Yuri, the trainer!'

Clouseau pulled off the killer's mask. It was Yuri, the trainer for the French football team.

'Oooooh!' cried the crowd. The people from the newspapers left Dreyfus and ran to Clouseau.

'Gluant was nothing!' Yuri said angrily. 'I did all the work. I found the players. I decided the way to play. He took everything from me and now he's dead.'

Ponton turned to Clouseau and asked, 'But how did you know the killer was Yuri?'

'Ponton, you must remember. You were there,' said Clouseau. 'Mrs Yu said, "Why am I here? I'm busy! The killer used Chinese herbs to make the poison dart. You must look for football trainers. They have to know about Chinese herbs!"'

'And she was right,' Clouseau continued. 'Every trainer of the French football team must know about Chinese herbs.'

'And Bizu?' someone asked.

'Very easy,' said Clouseau. 'Yuri wanted to kill Gluant, and Bizu knew about it. Bizu said to Yuri, "Pay me money or I will talk to the police." Yuri didn't want to pay Bizu anything. Instead he killed him!'

Yuri looked very angry. He looked at Xania.

'No, Yuri,' said Clouseau. 'Xania isn't dead. But you wanted her to die. You helped her a long time ago, before she met Bizu and Gluant. But she forgot you. That's why you wanted to kill her … The case is closed!'

Dreyfus pushed through the crowd until he reached Clouseau.

'Thank you, Inspector Clouseau. You have followed my instructions exactly,' said Dreyfus. Then he turned to Yuri and said, 'Now, give me the Pink Panther.'

'What?' Yuri said angrily. 'I don't care about that stupid diamond. It's nothing to me!'

'He doesn't have the diamond,' Clouseau said.

'He doesn't have the diamond? The killer doesn't have the diamond!' Dreyfus couldn't believe it.

'No,' said Clouseau, 'Xania has the Pink Panther. There in her bag!'

'Let me see,' said Dreyfus. He took Xania's bag. Then he threw everything in the bag onto a table. There was some make-up, some money and an old ticket – but no Pink Panther.

'Sorry, Clouseau, no diamond!' said Dreyfus, happy at last.

Clouseau walked to the table and picked up the bag. He took out a small knife and cut it open. There, between the inside and the outside of the bag, was the Pink Panther!

'Oooooh!' cried the crowd again.

'Yes, I have the diamond,' said Xania. 'A few hours before the match, Gluant asked me, "Will you be my wife?" I said yes and he said, "The Pink Panther is yours."'

'But Inspector, how did you know she had the diamond?' asked Ponton.

'It was easy, Ponton. I was looking at a photo of my arrest at the airport,' Clouseau explained. 'I saw something in that photo – Xania's bag in the x-ray machine. I made the photo bigger. In the bag was the Pink Panther.'

'Well done!' someone shouted.

'Well done, Clouseau!' another person shouted.

Clouseau looked around the room. He was surprised and very happy – more people started to shout, 'Well done, Clouseau!'

Dreyfus, of course, wasn't cheering. He was angry. He was so angry he wanted to hit Clouseau. Renard had to hold him back!

But soon everyone in the room was cheering and shouting, 'Well done, Clouseau!'

Epilogue
The Medal of Honour

A few days later, a large crowd of people were sitting and waiting outside the President's Palace. Clouseau and Ponton were sitting in front of the crowd. A band started to play.

Then the President of France started to speak. He talked about Clouseau and Ponton and their wonderful work. Then he said, 'In the name of France, I give the Medal of Honour to the brilliant Inspector Jacques Clouseau. For the people of France, he will always be the Pink Panther detective!'

Everyone shouted and cheered. And Clouseau and Ponton gave each other a big smile – they were so happy.

THE PINK PANTHER ™

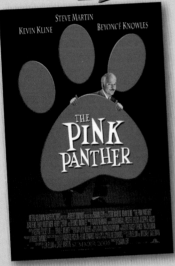

The Pink Panther appeared in 2006. It was popular because there were a lot of famous stars in the film. It was also very funny because of Inspector Clouseau and all the stupid things he does.

Peter Sellers

Did you know there was another film called *The Pink Panther*? It appeared in 1964 and Peter Sellers, a British star, played Inspector Clouseau. That film was also about the theft of a famous diamond – the Pink Panther. Inspector Clouseau goes to Italy and looks everywhere for the diamond except in the right place.

Peter Sellers became very famous as Clouseau and made five Pink Panther films.

> Have you seen any of the Pink Panther films with Peter Sellers?
>
> Have you seen *The Pink Panther* with Steve Martin?
>
> What kind of films make you laugh?

Did you know ... ?

Only two of the five films with Peter Sellers were about the Pink Panther diamond – *The Pink Panther* and *The Return of the Pink Panther*.

The diamond is called the Pink Panther because …

- it is pink.
- it has a small flaw inside. The flaw looks like a jumping panther.

The Pink Panther music is by Henry Mancini. He wrote music for many films and for TV, but the Pink Panther music is the most famous.

Do you know the Pink Panther music? Sing it to your partner.

Blake Edwards was the director of the Pink Panther films with Peter Sellers. For *The Pink Panther* he wanted something special for the start of the film. He asked two cartoonists, David DePatie and Fritz Feleng, to think of something – and the Pink Panther cartoon was born!

Steve Martin saw the Peter Sellers Pink Panther films when he was a young man. He loved them so much, he often copied Clouseau for his friends at university.

What do these words mean? You can use a dictionary.
theft flaw panther
director cartoon
cartoonist

STAR FILE

Name: Steve Martin (Inspector Clouseau)
Born: 14 August 1945, Waco, Texas, USA
Other films: *Shopgirl, Father of the Bride, Cheaper by the Dozen* and many others
Facts:

- He is a fantastic banjo player. He has won a Grammy award for his music.
- He loves art and owns works by Edward Hopper, Georgia O'Keefe, Pablo Picasso and many other artists.
- He met Peter Sellers once in Hawaii in 1980, but they never worked together.

STAR FILE

Name: Beyoncé Knowles (Xania)
Born: 4 September 1981, Houston, Texas, USA
Other films: *Dreamgirls, Austin Powers, The Fighting Temptations*
Facts:

- She was the main singer and writer of Destiny's Child. The group got a star on the Hollywood Walk of Fame in 2006.
- Her family work closely with her. Her father is her manager. Her mother makes her clothes. Her sister, Solange, also sings.

The biggest actors have stars on Hollywood's 'Walk of Fame'.

STAR FILE

Name: Jean Reno (Ponton)
Born: 30 July 1948, Casablanca, Morocco
Other films: *The Da Vinci Code, Mission Impossible, Godzilla* and many others
Facts:
• He left Morocco in 1967. He changed his name from Juan Moreno to Jean Reno.
• He said 'no' to the role of Agent Smith in *The Matrix*.
• He can speak French, English, Spanish and Italian.

STAR FILE

Name: Emily Mortimer (Nicole)
Born: 1 December 1971, London, UK
Other films: *Match Point, Scream 3, Bright Young Things*
Facts:
• She studied English and Russian at Oxford University.
• She found the role of Nicole in *The Pink Panther* more difficult than her role in *Match Point*.

Who is your favourite film star and why?

Do you know any interesting facts about him or her?

What do these words mean? You can use a dictionary.
banjo   award   art   artist   manager   actor   role

Diamonds are

Diamonds are the most expensive jewels in the world. They are also the hardest material in the world. For thousands of years people have used diamonds – to look rich and beautiful. But what else do you know about them?

Where do diamonds come from?

Diamonds appear in very deep and very hot places in the Earth (about 80 kilometres down). People have to build mines to get diamonds out of the Earth.

A diamond mine

How do you value a diamond?

The four Cs help people to value a diamond:

Clarity How clear is the diamond? Completely clear diamonds are the most expensive.

Colour Diamonds can be many colours – yellow, green, blue, brown, pink, red, orange, black … But the most popular diamonds have no colour at all.

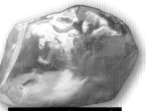
An uncut diamond

Cut Uncut stones don't look very special. Cut stones allow the light through and look brilliant and beautiful. You have to use a diamond to cut a diamond – nothing else will work!

Carat A carat is about 0.25g. The biggest, heaviest diamonds are the most expensive.

Have you ever seen a really big diamond?
Where did you see it? Do you like diamonds?

forever!

What is the biggest diamond in the world?
Cullinan I - also called The Star of Africa – is the biggest cut diamond in the world. It weighs 530.2 carats and has 74 faces. You can see it in the Tower of London – it was a gift to King Edward VII.

Cullinan I

How old are diamonds?
Most diamonds are about 3.3 billion years old. Some are even older than the Earth – they came to the Earth from space!

What do you think of the fashion for 'Bling'?

What about the 'Bling'?
Bling is a hip-hop word for expensive jewels and for a rich way of life. It started as a Jamaican street word for the sound in cartoons when light comes off a diamond – BLING-BLING!

A rapper called B.G. was the first to use the word. A song called 'Bling-bling' appeared on his CD in 1999. After that everyone was using the word *Bling*! And many people copied the fashion for lots of jewels and expensive things. Some rappers even have diamonds in their teeth.

What do these words mean? You can use a dictionary.
jewel material Earth mine value space cartoon

53

Chapters 1-4

Before you read
Use your dictionary for these questions.

1 Complete the sentences with these verbs. Put the verbs into the simple past.
   score   shoot   kiss   cheer
   a) The killer ... the man with a gun.
   b) The football player ... three goals.
   c) Everyone ... when the team won the match.
   d) The young man took the girl in his arms and ... her.

2 Match the words with the definitions.
   a) crowd   **i**   this person gives instructions to a sports team
   b) coach   **ii** it covers a window and stops the light
   c) honour   **iii** a very big group of people
   d) curtain   **iv** it is very hard, expensive and beautiful
   e) diamond   **v**   you have to do something special to get this

3 Complete the sentences with these words.
   case   suspect   deputy   poison dart
   a) The detective was working on a very important ... .
   b) He killed the man with a ... .
   c) A young woman hated the dead man. She was a ... .
   d) The detective told his ... to question the killer.

4 Do you like detective stories? What stories do you know?

5 Read 'People and Places' on pages 4 and 5. Who do you think killed Yves Gluant?

After you read

6 Answer the questions.
   a) Which team won the match?
   b) Why does Bizu hate Gluant?
   c) What did the killer use to kill Gluant?
   d) Did Gluant go to China?
   e) Why was Xania angry with Gluant?

7 Why do you think Clouseau puts a hair in his desk?

Chapters 5-8

Before you read

8 Match the two columns. You can use your dictionary.

a)	The mask	i	man was going to shoot his gun.
b)	The masked	ii	every day to become strong.
c)	He cut	iii	to go through the glass.
d)	She used a cutter	iv	hid his face.
e)	The trainer	v	told his team to run fast.
f)	She trained	vi	the bread with a knife.

9 Guess the answers to these questions.
- a) Who will Clouseau question next?
- b) Who is going to die next?
- c) Where will Clouseau question Raymond Larocque?
- d) Will Dreyfus be happy about all the interest in Clouseau?

Now read chapters 5–8. Were your guesses right?

After you read

10 Are these sentences true or false? Correct the false sentences.
- a) Clouseau questions Bizu at the French football team building.
- b) Vainqueur liked working for Gluant.
- c) Bizu thinks Larocque wanted to kill Gluant.
- d) Larocque is richer after Gluant dies.
- e) Boswell catches the Masked Bandits.
- f) Dreyfus hides under Clouseau's desk.

11 Put these parts of the story in order.
- a) Yuri, the trainer, comes into the training room.
- b) Clouseau questions Bizu.
- c) Clouseau and Ponton question Vainqueur in the training room.
- d) Clouseau questions Mrs Yu.
- e) Boswell catches the Masked Bandits at Larocque's Casino.
- f) Clouseau questions Raymond Larocque in his flat.

12 Now who do you think the killer is? Why?

13 You work for a newspaper. Write a headline and a story about Clouseau and the Masked Bandits.

Chapters 9–Epilogue

Before you read

14 Complete the sentences with these words. You can use your dictionary.

x-ray machine   herb   arrested   swords

a) The cook used a special ... in the food.
b) The police ... the killer late last night.
c) In the past, people fought with ... , not guns.
d) They put the bag through the ... .

Now read chapters 9–Epilogue. Were you right?

After you read

15 Match the sentences with the places.

a) Ponton and Clouseau discuss the Gluant case.
b) Ponton and Clouseau follow Xania.
c) Clouseau has dinner with Xania.
d) Clouseau hides some hamburgers in his pocket.
e) Clouseau looks at the news on the Internet.
f) Dreyfus arrests Doctor Li How Pang.

i   in the Waldorf Astoria hotel
ii   at the President's Palace
iii at the airport
iv   in Clouseau's flat
v   in New York
vi   by the river Seine

16 Answer the questions.

a) What is the man in the old building cutting?
b) What happens to Clouseau's hair?
c) Why do the police arrest Clouseau at the airport?
d) Why does Dreyfus think Doctor Pang is the killer?
e) Why did Dreyfus make Clouseau an Inspector?
f) Who does Clouseau arrest? Why?
g) Who has the Pink Panther? Why?

17 What do you think will happen to Clouseau next?

18 Would you like to be a detective? Why? / Why not?